ILFRACOMBE

HISTORY TOUR

First published 2020

Amberley Publishing
The Hill, Stroud,
Gloucestershire, GL5 4EP
www.amberley-books.com

Copyright © Peter Christie &
Graham Hobbs, 2020
Map contains Ordnance Survey data
© Crown copyright and database
right [2020]

The right of Peter Christie &
Graham Hobbs to be identified as the
Authors of this work has been asserted
in accordance with the Copyrights,
Designs and Patents Act 1988.

ISBN 978 1 3981 0066 4 (print)
ISBN 978 1 3981 0067 1 (ebook)

British Library Cataloguing in
Publication Data.
A catalogue record for this book is
available from the British Library.

Origination by Amberley Publishing.
Printed in Great Britain.

INTRODUCTION

Ilfracombe is a town with a fascinating and somewhat unusual history and a selection of books have been written about it, but if you really want to understand its past you need to walk around its harbour and streets. The town has a rich range of buildings that reflect its history as one of Britain's premier tourist resorts, varying from grand hotels to everyday houses and shops – all of which have played a part in creating the Ilfracombe we know today.

This small book is an effort to guide and inform both locals and visitors alike around some of the interesting parts of Ilfracombe. It cannot, of course, cover every building but anyone following our route should learn something about the town they are living in or visiting. One thing that has become clear is that Ilfracombe has experienced just as many changes as other small towns throughout Britain. Businesses have come and gone while buildings have been remodelled to cater for new needs. Not all of these changes have been welcomed but history never stands still and what might have been seen as a vulgar new addition to the streetscape when built has now, with the passing of the years, become a much-loved structure.

Ilfracombe escaped the worst excesses of the 1960s for the most part and it still retains the feeling of a friendly small town, with breathtaking views around almost every corner. Recent government diktats have ordered that Ilfracombe accommodate 1,400-plus new houses over the next twelve years which, if built, will mean the town will change again; whether for the better or worse is impossible to tell but whatever happens the historic core of the town will remain. This book is a guide to some of that history – we hope you enjoy it.

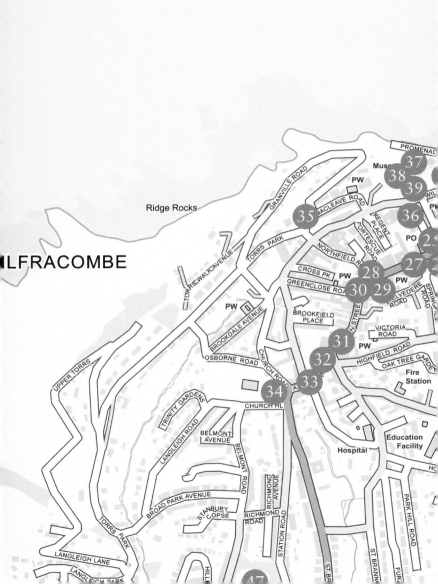

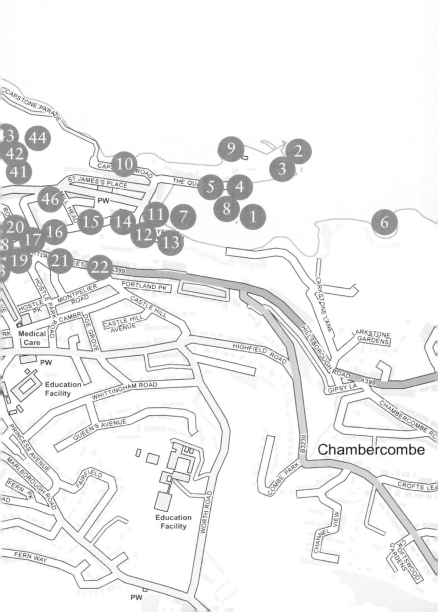

KEY

1. Ilfracombe Harbour
2. P&A Campbell's Steamers
3. Ilfracombe Pier
4. Great Gale at the Pier
5. Ilfracombe Harbour
6. Raparee Cove
7. *Co-operator No. 2*
8. Ilfracombe Fishermen
9. St Nicholas' Chapel
10. Capstone Road
11. Admiral Rodney Inn
12. Broad and Fore Street Junction
13. Broad and Fore Street Passageway
14. Ebrington Arms
15. Fore Street
16. Fore Street
17. Mr Cole's Shop
18. Cravings
19. Fire at the Junction
20. Candar Centre
21. Candar Centre Fire
22. Portland Street
23. J. Butler's Wine Shop
24. High Street Clock Tower
25. High Street
26. The Embassy Cinema
27. Pancake Race
28. The Bunch of Grapes
29. Post Office
30. Devon and Cornwall Police Band
31. Church Street
32. Church Street
33. Alpha Boarding Establishment
34. Ilfracombe War Memorial
35. Ilfracombe Sea Bathing Company
36. Emmanuel Church
37. Ilfracombe Hotel
38. Ilfracombe Hotel
39. Ilfracombe Hotel
40. Promenade
41. Victoria Pavilion
42. Victoria Pavilion
43. The Capstone
44. The Capstone
45. The Waitress Race
46. Collingwood Hotel
47. Ilfracombe Station

1. ILFRACOMBE HARBOUR

Ilfracombe grew around its natural harbour and one of the earliest photographs of the area appeared in a book published in July 1878 entitled *Ilfracombe and the North Devon Coast* by W. Walters. The shot was taken by James Catford, a local photographer who was operating in the town from around 1869 to 1892 while Walters was the Ilfracombe correspondent of the local newspaper, the *North Devon Journal*.

2. P&A CAMPBELL'S STEAMERS

Early in its history the harbour was extended with a wooden pier, against which P&A Campbell's steamers once tied up and sent forth their hundreds of tourists. This picture shows the pier around 1900 with seven steamers tied up side to side, with passengers having to clamber from one to the other in order to disembark.

3. ILFRACOMBE PIER

Unfortunately, the pier was partly demolished during the Second World War to prevent its possible use by invading Nazis and had to be rebuilt in 1952 – as shown in this photograph. It was then refurbished again in 1975 and today plays host to many events and is still a hugely popular tourist attraction.

4. GREAT GALE AT THE PIER

Though the town is sheltered by surrounding hills, Ilfracombe was as open to storm damage as any other coastal town. In 1910 a huge gale led to a storm surge that caused much damage to the pier and the surrounding and buildings. Termed a 'tidal wave' at the time by newspaper reporters, it was actually caused by a combination of an unusually high tide allied with strong winds stemming from a huge area of low pressure in the Atlantic. A similar situation seems to have occurred in 1607 when both sides of the Bristol Channel were inundated.

5. ILFRACOMBE HARBOUR

As the central hub of the town the harbour always seems to be crowded whenever pictures are taken of it. The photograph here dates from around 1890 and shows a crowd of sailors and fishermen with a pair of horse-drawn vehicles, a scene replicated in our 2012 shot (inset), though the seamen have been replaced by tourists and the sailing boats are now represented by motor craft.

RAPAREE BATHING COVE, ILFRACOMBE. 2264

6. RAPAREE COVE

Just round the coast from the harbour is Raparee Cove, a small, sheltered beach that has provided a relatively safe bathing area for many years – and a subject for many postcards over the last 120 years. The cove is the site of the 1796 shipwreck of the *London*, which was possibly carrying gold and/or French soldiers or slaves from the West Indies.

7. CO-OPERATOR NO. 2

Not unexpectedly given its position and history, Ilfracombe has had a long connection with lifeboats, being able to trace its first such boat back to 1828. This 1886 photograph shows the newly built *Co-operator No. 2*, a horse-drawn man-powered lifeboat, on the harbour sands. A new lifeboat house was built for it in 1893, which remained in use until 1996.

NATIONAL LIFE BOAT INSTITUTION

JUNE 18 1866

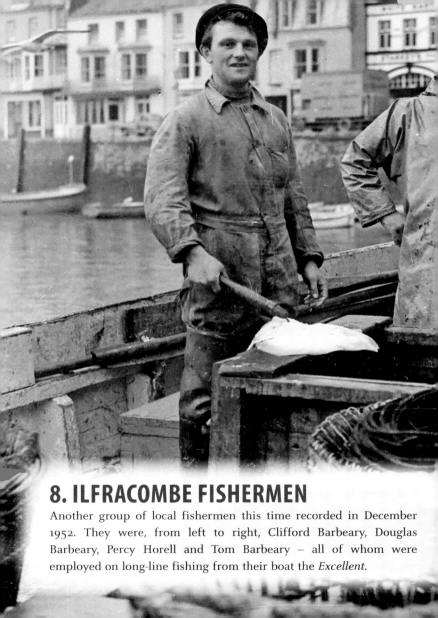

8. ILFRACOMBE FISHERMEN

Another group of local fishermen this time recorded in December 1952. They were, from left to right, Clifford Barbeary, Douglas Barbeary, Percy Horell and Tom Barbeary – all of whom were employed on long-line fishing from their boat the *Excellent*.

9. ST NICHOLAS' CHAPEL

The old pier and St Nicholas' Chapel (dating from at least the fifteenth century) are shown well in this shot from 1895. The wooden ketch in the foreground is the *Arabella* of Gloucester, which was wrecked on the Britton's Rock in the harbour in October 1895 and lost its four-man crew along with two local men.

10. CAPSTONE ROAD

The photograph here probably dates from around 1880 and shows just how bad and rundown some of the old houses in Ilfracombe were – this being Capstone Road looking down to the modern Sandpiper Inn. The same view today can only be recognised by the steepness of the road and the sharpness of the corner.

11. ADMIRAL RODNEY INN

The name of the Admiral Rodney Inn harks back to a very successful late eighteenth-century naval officer who, in his illustrious career, managed to destroy both Spanish and French fleets. The inn disappeared in 1915 and today the harbour can still be glimpsed at the end of the alley, but the area has now become very bland when compared to how atmospheric it used to be.

12. BROAD AND FORE STREET JUNCTION

Ilfracombe as a town is dynamic in the sense that buildings come and go or are refashioned for new uses. This photograph, with its wonderful wall of posters, gas lamp and rough road surface, records a building that once stood at the junction of Broad and Fore Streets, which was cleared to open up Quayfield Road.

A Bit of Old Ilfracombe

13. BROAD AND FORE STREET PASSAGEWAY

This close-up view of the passageway on the left of the previous picture shows why the thoroughfare needed to be widened. Both shots appear to date from around 1900.

14. EBRINGTON ARMS

Not all the old buildings in Fore Street have survived, however, including the Ebrington Arms (named after one of the titles borne by the local Earl Fortescue and his descendants). It was demolished in 1966 in order to widen the road, with the workmen involved having a last celebratory pint in its interior before they knocked it down.

15. FORE STREET

Further down Fore Street and the varied nature and date of the buildings is very apparent in this 1966 photograph – by which date the dreaded, though necessary, double-yellow lines had made their appearance.

16. FORE STREET

The name Fore Street is common in the South West and needless to say Ilfracombe has one. It is narrow, winding and full of atmosphere. Being a thoroughfare leading to the harbour it has always been busy, as this late nineteenth-century image displays. The steps to the right still remain today.

17. MR COLE'S SHOP

Where Fore Street meets Portland Street the tightly hemmed-in site has seen the development of narrow buildings, as seen in this 1890 shot where a Mr Cole was running a varied range of businesses including coal merchant, plumber, tin man, furniture dealer and ironmonger.

18. CRAVINGS

Given the constricted nature of the site, the only way to grow was upwards as proved by this 2012 picture. The 'welcoming' arch to the left is a recent addition to the street furniture.

19. FIRE AT THE JUNCTION

This site hasn't always been this peaceful, as seen in this image from August 1983 when a fire gutted the building, which then housed an amusement arcade.

20. CANDAR CENTRE

Following this disaster the area was totally rebuilt as the Candar Centre, which includes the Ilfracombe Library along with a blue plaque recording that 'On this site stood the Ilfracombe Arcade'.

21. CANDAR CENTRE FIRE

This fire had been preceded by another just two years before when the buildings opposite were badly affected, though their pleasing exterior brickwork was saved.

22. PORTLAND STREET

That the car rules our towns today is a truism, and towns have had to change to accommodate them. This late 1960s shot shows the top of a narrow Portland Street, where all the buildings fronting the road have been demolished in order to widen the carriageway and enable vehicles to move faster.

23. J. BUTLER'S WINE SHOP

The High Street is still the town's major shopping street, though its appearance has greatly altered since this photograph of the eastern end was taken around 1910 – when there was only horse-drawn traffic. The shop on the right once housed J. Butler's wine business but is now the St George public house – a nice example of historical continuity.

24. HIGH STREET CLOCK TOWER

Moving along the High Street and again the shops have changed from when this shot was taken in the last decade of the nineteenth century. The clock tower, completed in May 1874 under the supervision of local clockmaker Mr Thomas, still stands.

25. HIGH STREET

With pressure from out-of-town shops and the internet normal shops are now suffering, but empty shops are nothing new as this mid-1960s photograph of part of the High Street shows. Frontages above the shop windows are still much the same today.

Entire
FREEHOLD PROPERTY
SOLD BY
P.J.WILLIAMS
6. STRATTON ST.,W.1.
HYD. 4164/5

G. H. JONES

26. THE EMBASSY CINEMA

Ilfracombe was the first place in north Devon to see moving films in May 1897 when a 75-foot-long film was shown in the town hall by one Charles Hopward, with the town itself being used as the backdrop to a story being filmed by a cinematography crew only a few years later in 1912. The Embassy Cinema in High Street, which still operates today, was a late arrival, having opened in 1948 in what had been a church, which itself had only been opened nine years before.

27. PANCAKE RACE

Many towns have quirky events and this image from 1984 shows that year's fancy dress pancake race being staged in the High Street. Today Ilfracombe stages the 'Bird Man' contest where aspiring 'aviators' launch themselves from the pier in home-made 'flying machines' – with predictable results.

28. THE BUNCH OF GRAPES

The Bunch of Grapes public house with its arched windows is on the left of this 1930s photograph, including a wonderful display of old-style cars and buses and no yellow lines.

29. POST OFFICE

This nicely coloured picture dates from the late 1950s/early 1960s and was used in the town's publicity brochures of the time. The post office has now, as in so many towns, disappeared into a nearby supermarket – a victim of e-mails and mobile phones.

30. DEVON AND CORNWALL POLICE BAND

This 1980 image shows the Devon and Cornwall police band marching along the High Street, having just passed the old Independent chapel, which can trace its history back to 1728. Today it is the Lantern, run by the town council as a well-used community centre.

31. CHURCH STREET

The southern end of Church Street pictured around 1870, with two levels for the road and path. Today all the buildings have been completely altered, with the plate glass windows of modern shops replacing the small paned domestic windows of Victorian England.

32. CHURCH STREET

A bit further northwards along Church Street and although the general shape of the road is still recognisable, the buildings, path and road surfaces have all been greatly altered.

33. ALPHA BOARDING ESTABLISHMENT

This extraordinary building, which stands at the junction of Church Street and Wilder Road, was originally built as the Alpha Boarding Establishment. The unusual circular tower entrance makes the best and most eye-catching use of a rather constricted site. Refurbished a few years ago, the building now provides an exotic-looking entrance to the town.

34. ILFRACOMBE WAR MEMORIAL

The Ilfracombe war memorial is a handsome pillar topped with a figure of 'Winged Victory' standing at the entrance to the parish church of Holy Trinity. It records the names of 157 First World War and sixty-two Second World War dead from Ilfracombe and has provided the focus for Remembrance Day services since it was erected. Our photograph shows a 1960s service that has a variety of flags from different organisations on display.

35. ILFRACOMBE SEA BATHING COMPANY

This wonderfully simple yet well-proportioned building was erected by the Ilfracombe Sea Bathing Company in 1836 to provide both hot and cold baths and to exploit the 1820s hand-carved tunnels that led

down to the Tunnels Beaches, which was segregated into male and female sections up until 1905. The heavily laden coach in the picture was old fashioned even when this photograph was taken in 1896 and was laid on to cater mainly to tourists who wanted to go home and boast they had ridden on a stagecoach.

36. EMMANUEL CHURCH

One type of building that rarely changes, at least in its physical appearance, are churches. This 1951 image shows Emmanuel Church in Wilder Road. Designed in the then fashionable Gothic style by W. H. Gould for the town's Methodists, it was opened in 1898, having been built in just ten months.

37. ILFRACOMBE HOTEL

One building that has disappeared is the Ilfracombe Hotel, the massive building on the right of this image. It represented the last word in Victorian luxury on its opening in May 1867, having been designed by Mr Horne, a London architect. Today part of its site houses the Landmark Theatre, which, with its two cones, was called 'Madonna's bra' by local people.

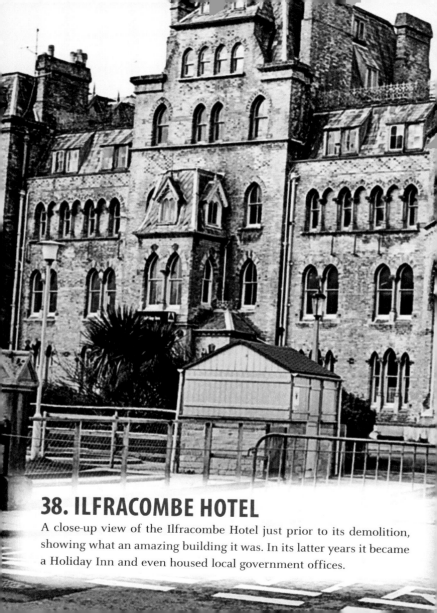

38. ILFRACOMBE HOTEL

A close-up view of the Ilfracombe Hotel just prior to its demolition, showing what an amazing building it was. In its latter years it became a Holiday Inn and even housed local government offices.

39. ILFRACOMBE HOTEL

Another shot of the hotel with a wishing well in front of it in this tourist publicity photograph.

FRACOMBE FROM BATTEN'S CORNE

40. PROMENADE

When visitors came to Ilfracombe they brought their best holiday clothes and paraded up and down the promenade to both see others and to be seen. Both of these Edwardian images demonstrate just how smart some of these outfits could be – and how packed the town was during the summer season.

41. VICTORIA PAVILION

Opened in 1888 on the lower slopes of the Capstone, the Victoria Pavilion was largely rebuilt following a disastrous fire in 1949. It had acted as a theatre for visiting acts for many years, but eventually became too costly to repair, so it was demolished in 1992 with the site being left as an open space.

42. VICTORIA PAVILION

Not only was the Pavilion a theatre, it also provided sheltered seats for visitors, as pictured here – though whether the umbrella was to keep the rain or sun off is uncertain. The gentleman in the uniform is assumed to be a ticket collector as seats were not free.

43. THE CAPSTONE

The Capstone has been important in Ilfracombe's history, providing as it does a spectacular viewpoint over the town – if you can make the steep climb up the zig-zag pathway, which was opened in April 1894. The Parade at the foot of the hill dates from September 1843, with the funds to develop it being raised by a public subscription in the town. This old print shows the Parade on its opening. Note the presence of a wheeled bathing hut on the beach in which Victorian swimmers would have changed. Its inauguration was celebrated with a regatta and it has been suggested that this marked the start of mass tourism to Ilfracombe.

44. THE CAPSTONE

The Capstone has always acted as a natural display space as is evident in this 1909 photograph where local schoolchildren have been marshalled to spell out 'Empire Day'. As shown in the second photograph (overleaf), the exercise was repeated two years later to mark the coronation of George V and Queen Mary – doubtless two events that few of the participants would ever forget.

45. THE WAITRESS RACE

One of the highlights of the annual Ilfracombe carnival was the 'Waitress Race'. Woman employed in local hotels were allowed time off to take part in this light-hearted event, with prizes being presented by the mayor and mayoress of the day. Winners were, of course, a good advertisement for their hotels. This particular race took place in 1956.

46. COLLINGWOOD HOTEL

Ilfracombe was one of the most popular tourist destinations in the Victorian and Edwardian periods, with many grand hotels catering to the tens of thousands of visitors who arrived every year. This postcard shows the much-loved Collingwood Hotel, which has now been demolished and replaced with a Wetherspoon's public house. It does, however, still bear the name The Admiral Collingwood.

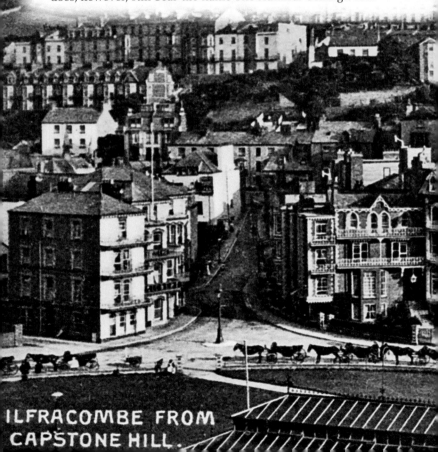

ILFRACOMBE FROM CAPSTONE HILL.

47. ILFRACOMBE STATION

Most visitors would have arrived by train. The railway reached Ilfracombe in 1874 but disappeared in 1970 following Dr Beecham's radical cutback in the number of railway lines. Many have said that this sounded the death knell of tourism in the town, but the appeal of cheap foreign package holidays and the vagaries of British weather probably had as much to do with it as the loss of the train. Our photograph shows Ilfracombe station just prior to its closure.